DIGITAL DEFENCE - 1

A STUDENT'S GUIDE TO SCAMS AND SAFETY

Mr. Ray

Copyright © <Published Year> <Author Name>

Made with ❤ on the Notion Press Platform

www.notionpress.com

Gift it to your family & friends and help everyone stay safe !!

This Book is Now Available on Amazon and Flipkart.

Follow us on Instagram @DigitalDefenceBook

Contents

Acknowledgments

This book began as a simple idea — to help people, especially students and families, stay safe in a world that's increasingly connected, yet increasingly dangerous. What I didn't expect was how many people would guide, inspire, and support me along the way.

I'm grateful to the many individuals who shared their stories, insights, and experiences. Your voices helped shape the heart of this book.

Thank you to educators, cybercrime professionals, and digital safety advocates who work every day to protect others — your efforts inspired much of what's written here.

To my family and friends, your encouragement kept me grounded.

Most of all, this book is for every young person who's ever felt confused, scared, or unsure online. May these pages give you clarity, confidence, and the power to protect not just yourself — but others too.

With sincere gratitude,
Mr. Ray

Welcome to the Digital Defence

Understanding the World of Online Scams

Not long ago, staying safe meant locking your door, keeping your wallet close, and avoiding dark alleys.

Today? It means thinking before you click, before you tap, and even before you trust a voice on the other end of a call.

Because scams don't always come in the form of masked robbers or stolen wallets.
 Now, they show up as:

"Congratulations! You've won an iPhone."
 "Your bank account will be blocked unless you verify now."
 "Hi, I'm a police officer. This is a recorded call."

They appear through text messages, emails, video calls, fake websites, DMs on Instagram, or links in WhatsApp groups. And the truth is — no one is too smart to be fooled.

Yes, even you.

So, What Exactly Is a Digital Scam?

A digital scam (also called a cyber scam) is when someone tries to trick you online to:

- Steal your money
- Steal your personal information
- Take control of your social media, email, or bank accounts
- Make you do something through fear, emotion, or pressure

And they're getting smarter — using fake uniforms, cloned websites, AI-generated voices, and messages that look *so real*, even adults fall for them.

But Why Should *Students* Learn This?

Because scammers don't just target working people or the elderly anymore.

They target:

- Students on Instagram
- Teens joining Telegram or gaming groups
- School WhatsApp groups
- Even students' parents and teachers, through them

You are often the first line of defence for your family.
If you can spot a scam, you can stop it — not just for yourself, but for those around you.

Types of Digital Scams You'll Read About in This Book:

Here's a quick look at the most common (and dangerous) types of scams I'll cover — through real stories and characters like you.

1. Phishing Scams

You get a fake link or login page that looks just like Instagram, Gmail, or your bank. You enter your details, and boom — they have full access.

We'll show you how to spot a fake link in Chapter 1: The Link That Looked Legit.

2. Digital Arrest & Police Impersonation

You receive a WhatsApp call from someone in a police uniform saying you're "under digital surveillance." They ask for money to clear your name.

This real scam has cost people crores — even senior citizens.

3. Fake Job, Scholarship & Competition Offers

You get an email saying you've been selected for a prize, job, or award — but first, you need to pay a "processing fee."

We cover this in Chapter 8: The Online Job Scam.

4. Love, Grooming & Honeytrap Scams

Someone flirts with you online, builds trust, and slowly pressures you into sending photos or money — then turns on you.

You'll meet Rudra, Riya, Aarav, and others who faced this in Chapters 2,3 & 13.

5. Ponzi Schemes & Investment Traps

You invest in "guaranteed returns" through Telegram groups. At first, you earn — then it all disappears.

Learn about DB Stock and how real people lost crores in Chapter 6.

Why This Book Exists?

Because schools teach us how to solve math problems —
...but not how to spot a scam link.
Because we learn history —
...but not what to do when a fake police officer video calls us.
Because the internet is part of our lives —
...and scammers are hiding in every corner of it.

This book is here to help you to understand how scams work, see real examples, protect yourself and your family and help you know what to do if you ever get trapped.

Let's begin.
Turn the page, and meet Aarav — who gets panicked due to fake news.

1. Fake News: The Paper Leak Panic

(When Fake News Creates Real Stress)

Characters:

- *Aarav* – 16, preparing for his CBSE board exams
- *Nidhi* – his classmate, calm but easily influenced by friends
- *Class WhatsApp Group* – where the panic begins
- *Mr. Sinha* – their maths teacher, trusted and experienced

[Scene: 9:30 PM – Aarav's bedroom. Books are open, his calculator is nearby. He's reviewing formulas when his phone buzzes. Again. And again.]

 Class Group (Forwarded Message):
 *BREAKING NEWS*
MATHS PAPER LEAKED – PDF circulating on Telegram and WhatsApp
Exam might be CANCELLED. Sources say board is meeting now.
Check attached file! Match the questions!

Aarav (muttering):
"What the... paper leaked? No way."

[He taps the PDF, heart racing. The file opens. It's a set of questions that look... familiar. Too familiar.]

Aarav:
 "Wait a second... isn't this our last year's sample paper?"

[Message pings again. This time from Nidhi.]

Nidhi:
 Hey... saw the group? Is it true? Should we still study?

Aarav:
 "I'm not sure. The questions look real but kinda recycled."

Nidhi:
 "My mom is telling me to sleep early — says it'll be cancelled anyway. This is so confusing!"

Aarav:
 "Let's not assume anything. I'll text Mr. Sinha."

[Aarav hesitates, then sends a message to Mr. Sinha.]

Aarav:
 Sir, is the maths paper really leaked? Everyone's saying it's cancelled tomorrow.

[No reply. Tension builds. Aarav scrolls Twitter. Nothing. CBSE website — no announcement. He decides to keep revising.]

[Next Morning – Outside school. Buzzing students. Nervous energy everywhere.]

Nidhi (walking beside Aarav):
 "I barely slept. My cousin messaged at 2 AM — said the board would reschedule."

Aarav:
 "Still nothing official. Let's see what Sir says."

[In the school corridor, Mr. Sinha gathers the students before the exam starts.]

Mr. Sinha (calm, firm):
 "Good morning, everyone. I know there's been a flood of messages about a leaked paper. Let me be clear — the exam is not cancelled. That 'leak' circulating online? It's fake. The PDF was based on last year's paper, edited to confuse students. There is no official notice, and CBSE has confirmed that the exam is on."

[Gasps. Relief. Some embarrassment.]

Nidhi (quietly):
 "I really thought it was real."

Aarav:
Yes.... "Lesson learned."

❓ What Just Happened?

Aarav and his classmates got swept up in a fake news storm — a classic case of exam panic + social media = confusion.

Someone created a fake PDF (possibly edited from older questions) and labeled it a "leak."
Others forwarded it without verifying, and students across groups assumed it was true.

 ## Lesson: How to Handle Exam Fake News

1. Check the Source — Not Just the Message

- Is it from the board website (cbse.gov.in or your state board)?
- Is it posted on official school communication channels?
- Has it been confirmed by your teacher or principal?

If not — it's probably just noise.

2. Don't Trust PDFs or Screenshots Without Context

Many "leaked" question papers are:

- From previous years
- Taken from coaching centre mock tests

- Edited to look real

Note that scammers may also charge money for these fake papers.

---

3. Don't Be the Forwarder

Forwarding unverified news — even to help — only adds to the panic.

Before you hit "send," ask:

- Is this real?
- Will this help or stress people out?
- Have I confirmed it from a reliable source?

---

4. Focus on What You Can Control

During exam season:

- Mute class groups at night if needed
- Stick to a trusted routine
- If in doubt, call your teacher or school admin directly
- Avoid being glued to Telegram/WhatsApp "leak" channels — many of them are traps

Final Thought:

Scammers and trolls know exactly when students are most vulnerable — exam time.
They feed off fear, panic, and last-minute confusion.

But you're smarter now.
Because real toppers don't just solve questions — they ignore distractions.

Remember that focus beats fake. Every single time.

Chapter Focus:

Fake news is not always about exam leaks or prize scams.
Sometimes, it spreads fear, hate, or panic — and in the worst cases, it leads to violence and even death.

Some of the most disturbing effects of unchecked misinformation includes:

- Fake communal violence videos shared to trigger riots
- False earthquake warnings that caused stampedes and fear
- Child-kidnapping rumors that led to people being beaten or killed — like the horrifying case in Assam

 Real Example: The Assam Lynching (2018)

Two young men — Nilotpal and Abhijit — were travelling in a village in Karbi Anglong, Assam.
   They were attacked and killed by a mob after fake messages circulated on social media claiming that child kidnappers were roaming nearby.

The video of the lynching went viral. But the truth?
 They were innocent artists, not kidnappers.

The killers didn't know them.
 They only believed the fake news they received.

Why It Happens:

People forward shocking videos or texts without checking.
 Fake news creators:

- Edit old or unrelated videos
- Add dramatic captions like "Breaking!" or "Urgent!"
  Use emotion (fear, anger, hate) to spread fast

Many of these messages:

- Show violence from other countries and claim it's local
- Spread communal hatred, trying to turn people against each other
- Claim natural disasters (like earthquakes, floods) that don't exist

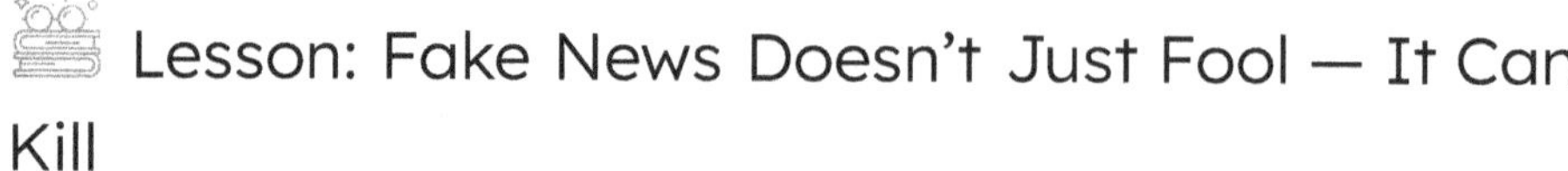 Lesson: Fake News Doesn't Just Fool — It Can Kill

❌ Don't believe just because:

- "It has a video"
- "It came from a family group"
- "It was forwarded 50 times"
- "Everyone is talking about it"

☑ Do this instead:

- Reverse search images or videos using Google Lens or TinEye
- Look for the same news on reputed news websites
- Ask: *What could happen if I share this and it's not true?*

Remember:

You have the power to stop the chain.
All it takes is one smart pause before forwarding.

2. The Honey Trap Scam

<u>(When Love Is Just a Lie With a Plan)</u>

Characters:

- *Rudra* – 16, quiet, introverted, curious about dating
- *"Simran"* – a mysterious girl who messages him online
- *Ishaan* – Rudra's classmate, more skeptical and alert
- *Rudra's Father* – appears later

[Scene: Rudra is in bed late at night, scrolling through Instagram when a new message request pops up.]

Simran (DM):
 Hey... I saw your profile. You look kinda cute.

 Mind if we talk a little? 🙈

Rudra (surprised):
 Uh... sure. You're... Simran?

Simran:
 Yeah. From Delhi. Just bored. You?

[Over the next few days, they chat constantly. She flirts, compliments him, asks about his school, his life. Rudra feels seen for the first time.]

Simran:
*You seem different. Guys don't usually talk this nicely.
You ever had a girlfriend?*

Rudra:
No... not really. You?

Simran:
Maybe you could be the first. Wanna see what I look like?

[She sends a semi-blurry photo of a girl. Rudra assumes it's real. Then comes the hook.]

Simran:
Can you send me something cute too? Like a shirtless selfie? No face — just for fun. 🙂
I promise no one will see. Cross my heart.

[Rudra hesitates. Feels nervous. But excited. He sends a cropped photo. Minutes later... everything changes.]

Simran (new message):
*Thanks, Rudra. Now listen — send me ₹5,000 or I'll post this photo to your school group.
I have your followers list. Don't test me.*

Rudra (panicked):
What!? You said it was private!

Simran:
This is called honey trapping, baby. Pay up or get exposed.

[The next day, Rudra tells Ishaan, shaken. Ishaan doesn't laugh. He listens.]

Ishaan:
 You didn't do anything wrong. But you've got to act fast.
 First — block her.
 Second — tell your dad or someone at school. You're not the first victim.

[Together, they talk to Rudra's father. The account is reported, the scammer is blocked, and no leak ever happens.]

What Just Happened?

Rudra was honey trapped — a scam where someone pretends to show romantic or sexual interest, lures you into sending personal photos or videos, and then blackmails you for money.

Scammers often:

- Use fake photos or stolen identities
- Act sweet and romantic for days or weeks
- Create a false sense of trust
- Turn aggressive the moment they get what they want

It happens to boys and girls, often in silence and shame.

Lesson: How to Recognize & Respond to Honey Trap Scams

1. Flirting from a Stranger = Red Flag

If someone random says:

"You're cute", "I never message guys first", or "Let's keep this secret"

...it's likely a trap, not love.

2. Never Share Personal or Intimate Photos

Even if they:

- Don't show their own face
- Say they won't screenshot
- Swear they'll delete after seeing

Once it's sent, you lose control.

3. The Switch Is Fast

The moment you send something, the tone changes:

- "Pay me or I'll post this"
- "You have 1 hour or your friends will see"

This is digital blackmail, and it's illegal.

4. You Must Tell Someone

- Because shame protects scammers.

Telling a parent, teacher, counselor, or friend breaks their power.

Remember that you're not in trouble. You're in need of help. And you'll get it.

5. Never Pay. Block & Report Instead.

Paying once won't stop them — it just proves you're scared.
Instead:

- Take screenshots of threats
- Block the scammer
- Report it. (Check chapter 19)

☑ How to Stay Safe:

- Set accounts to private
- Don't accept unknown follow or friend requests
- Don't move conversations to WhatsApp or Telegram without knowing the person
- Never respond to blackmail — respond to it by reporting

Support friends going through it — don't judge, don't gossip

🧠 Remember:

Just because someone says "I like you" doesn't mean they respect you.

Real care never demands your photos. Or your silence. Or your money.

If someone pretends to love you just to trap you — that's not love. That's a crime.

3. The Honey Trap Scam - Part 2

(When the Trap Targets the Adults Too)

Characters:

- *Rudra* – 16, previously honey-trapped, now more aware
- *Rudra's Father* – senior employee at a tech firm, respected and responsible
- *"Pooja"* – the scammer, pretending to be a freelance journalist
- *Ishaan* – Rudra's friend, tech-smart and supportive

[Scene: One week after Rudra escaped his own honey trap. He's at home studying when he notices his father smiling at his phone.]

Rudra:
 Papa, who are you texting? You look way too happy for a workday.

Father (smiling):
 Ah... just a friend I met online. She's a journalist — name's Pooja. We connected over LinkedIn after a webinar.

Rudra (instantly alert):
 Wait... Pooja? Online? From where?

Father:
 Mumbai. She said she loved my talk on AI ethics and

wanted to interview me. But now we talk casually too. She's quite charming, actually.

[Rudra walks over and sees the messages — flirty emojis, compliments, selfies (nothing explicit, but suspiciously glamorous). Then comes the kicker:]

Pooja (text):
   You're so brilliant. I've never felt this connected to someone so quickly. 🩶
   By the way... what kind of security does your company use for cloud backups? Asking for research 🙈

Rudra (serious now):
 Papa... I need to talk to you. This... this is exactly how I got trapped last week.

Father (confused):
  But she's so respectful. She hasn't asked for anything wrong.

Rudra:
 Not *yet*. But she's building trust — making you feel special. That's the setup. Then she asks for "small" info. Next could be internal documents, staff names, or system logins.

[He shows his father screenshots of *similar corporate honey trap scams* — where fake profiles were used to extract company secrets or even plant spyware.]

Father (quiet now):
You really think she's not real?

Rudra:
Let's reverse search her photo.

[They use a reverse image tool — her photo shows up on multiple "model" profiles under different names.]

Father (shaken):
She's fake...

Rudra:
 Yes. And you didn't fall for it — but you almost did. Let's report it. And maybe you can warn your team too.

❓ What Just Happened?

Rudra's father was being honey-trapped through professional flattery and mild flirtation — not for money, but for company secrets. This is corporate honey trapping, where scammers target professionals, often men, and trick them into:

- Sharing confidential documents
- Clicking spyware links
- Giving access to internal systems

The tactic is the same:

- Build trust
- Make it feel emotional or flattering

- Slowly ask for things — pretending it's innocent

📚 Lesson: Adults Get Trapped Too — And You Can Help Them

1. Honey Traps Are Getting Smarter

They don't just ask for photos anymore. They:

- Pretend to be reporters, HRs, or researchers
- Use professional platforms like LinkedIn or email
- Mix personal charm with small, "harmless" questions

2. Manipulation Works at Any Age

Adults might believe:

- "I'm too experienced to be fooled"
- "She's just friendly"
- But everyone — even smart professionals — can fall for digital attention.

  It's not about foolishness. It's about trust. And trust can be used wrongly.

3. Information = Currency

Even if they don't ask for money, they may want:

- Employee databases
- System structures
- Password habits
- Files marked "confidential"

This info can be sold or used for cyberattacks on companies.

4. As a Student, You Can Educate Your Parents

- Help them recognize suspicious behavior
- Teach them about reverse image search
- Encourage them to talk if they feel "off" about someone online

5. What to Do If You Suspect a Honey Trap:

- Stop all communication
- Report the profile (LinkedIn, WhatsApp, Instagram, etc.)
- Alert your company's cybersecurity or HR team (if work is involved)
- Don't feel embarrassed — feel smart for spotting it

 Chapter Focus:

In the previous part of this chapter, we saw how Rudra's father was being tricked by someone pretending to be a friendly journalist, slowly pushing him to reveal work-related information.
 Luckily, Rudra spotted the trap in time.

But in real life, honeytrap scams don't always end safely. Sometimes, they lead to leaked secrets, arrests, and even jail time.

📌 Real Case: BrahMos Engineer Trapped & Convicted

In a recent and shocking case, Nishant Agarwal, a senior systems engineer at BrahMos Aerospace (India's leading missile research and development facility), was sentenced to life imprisonment for leaking sensitive missile data to Pakistan's intelligence agency, ISI.

🔍 How did it happen?

- He was reportedly approached online by a woman on Facebook, who claimed to be a defence enthusiast.
- They began chatting regularly. She earned his trust over time, appearing interested in his work and flattering him.

- Eventually, he shared classified information — thinking it was innocent, or maybe out of emotional attachment.

But this "woman" was actually part of a honeytrap operation run by Pakistani spies.

The result?
  He was caught, charged under the Official Secrets Act, and sentenced to 14 years of rigorous imprisonment.

This case shocked the nation and proved that honeytraps aren't just scams — they can be acts of espionage.

In Rudra's Words (Story Continuation...)

[Scene: Rudra and his dad are sitting together. His father is silent, staring at his phone.]

Rudra:
  "Papa... still thinking about that Pooja account?"

Father:
  "Yes. I feel embarrassed. It all felt... harmless. Like someone just being nice."

Rudra (seriously):
  "Did you hear about that BrahMos engineer? Nishant Agarwal? Same thing. Flirty Facebook messages, emotional chats... but they weren't just friendly. They were spies."

Father:
"And he told them things? Important things?"

Rudra:
"He leaked national secrets. Maybe he didn't mean to. But it started the same way — a fake profile, fake interest, real damage."

Father (quietly):
"Now I understand why even simple chats can be dangerous."

☑ How to Stay Safe:

- Reverse image search anyone new who connects with you
- Don't talk about your work or school systems online
- Don't click unknown links or files in private chats
- Trust your gut — if something feels off, it probably is
- Set boundaries: Just because they're "nice" doesn't mean they're safe
- If you're unsure, talk to someone you trust — early is better than sorry

---

☑ Real Talk:

You don't have to be in defence or tech to be targeted.

You just need to:

- Be emotionally available

- Have something valuable (data, photos, credentials, secrets)
- Be online at the wrong time, with the wrong person

From Rudra's dad to Nishant Agarwal, honeytraps have no age limit and no easy warning sign.

But now you've seen behind the mask.

4. Sexting - The Risk Behind the Message

<u>(What Feels Private Can Spread Fast)</u>

Characters:

- *Aarohi* – 15, in her first relationship, curious and trusting
- *Karan* – her boyfriend, 16, pushes boundaries
- *Nikki* – Aarohi's friend who notices something's off
- *Aarohi's Sister* – older, open-minded, and supportive

[Scene: Aarohi is on her bed, chatting with Karan over WhatsApp.]

Karan:
 You trust me, right? Just one photo. Something cute. No one will see it — I swear.

Aarohi (typing slowly):
 I don't know... I feel weird about it.

Karan:
 You're overthinking. It's normal between people who like each other. I'd never share it. It's just for me.

[She hesitates. After pressure and repeated "it's just us" messages, she sends a cropped, slightly revealing photo — not nude, but private. A few days pass. Things feel fine.]

[Until Nikki messages her late at night.]

Nikki:
 Aarohi... someone in another class forwarded a screenshot. It looked like you. Did you send Karan something?

Aarohi (heart racing):
 Wait, what? WHAT!?

[Panic sets in. She opens her phone, messages Karan.]

Aarohi:
 Why is someone else sharing that photo?

Karan (typing... then leaves her on seen):
 Seen.

[The next morning, Aarohi tells her older sister. She expects anger. Instead, she finds support.]

Sister:
 Okay. First — breathe. I know you're scared. But listen carefully:
 You're not bad. You're not stupid.
 He broke your trust. *You didn't do anything wrong.*

Aarohi (teary):
But... everyone will think I'm "that girl." What do I do?

Sister:
We report it. We get the photo taken down. And we make sure you're safe — not ashamed.

[They talk to a teacher. The school responds. Karan is called in. Aarohi is never blamed — she's protected, and the situation is stopped before it spreads further.]

❓ What Just Happened?

Aarohi sent a private photo under pressure from someone she trusted. That photo was shared — without her permission — and it caused fear, panic, and shame.

This is what happens with sexting:

- It starts with trust
- Often involves pressure
- Ends with betrayal or exposure

And worst of all — the person who feels the most ashamed is often the victim, not the one who broke the trust.

 Lesson: Sexting Isn't "Romantic" — It's Risky

1. Once Sent, It's Not Yours Anymore

Even if you:

- Crop the face
- Use a filter
- Share "just with one person"

The moment it leaves your phone, you lose control of where it goes next.

> Trust can be broken. Screenshots can be taken. Regret hits fast.

2. Real Respect = No Pressure

If someone says:

- "If you loved me, you'd send it."
- "It's normal, everyone does it."
- "Just one — I won't show anyone."

That's not love.
 That's manipulation.

3. You Can Say No — And Still Be Strong

Saying no to a private photo doesn't make you boring or immature. It makes you smart, confident, and in control.

4. If It Happens — Don't Freeze in Fear

If your photo is leaked, or someone threatens you with one:

- Don't panic or hide
- Talk to a trusted adult immediately
- Report the account or platform
- Take screenshots as evidence

Most schools, police teams, and cyber cells take this very seriously now.

5. Support Friends Instead of Judging Them

If someone you know is affected:

- Don't spread it
- Don't make jokes
- Don't say "she deserved it"

Say:

"I'm here for you. Let's fix this."

Because they don't need punishment. They need protection.

☑ Red Flags to Watch For in Sexting Pressure:

- Repeated "just once" messages
- Using guilt, threats, or flattery
- Promises to delete after viewing
- No willingness to respect your "no"

- Ghosting you when you refuse

Remember:

You never need to prove love with a photo.
And if someone puts you in that position — they're not worth your trust.

Mistakes happen. But shame doesn't belong to you.
Courage starts when you speak. Strength begins when you
stop blaming yourself.

---

5. Phishing: The Link that Looked Legit

<u>(When One Click Almost Cost Everything)</u>

Characters:

- *Riya* – 14, excited and active on WhatsApp and Instagram
- *Aman* – her classmate and close friend, more logical and careful
- *"InstaGift Team"* – the fake account/scammer
- *Riya's Dad* – appears later

📲 Scene: Wednesday evening, just after school

Riya flopped onto the couch, pulled out her phone, and tapped open Instagram. She wasn't even looking for anything serious — just memes and reels. That's when she saw the DM.

> "Congratulations 🎉 🎉
> You've been selected in the *InstaGift Giveaway!*
> Claim your FREE iPhone 14 by clicking the link below.
> Only 10 winners chosen from India. Hurry!"

The account's profile pic had an Instagram logo, and the username was something like:
@instagift.official_winnerz

It *looked* legit enough. And she remembered entering some random giveaway a few weeks ago.

Riya (excitedly texting Aman):

Brooooo guess what!! I think I won something 

Aman:
Huh? What now?

Riya (screenshots the message):
LOOK

Aman (typing):
Wait wait wait. Don't click anything yet.

Riya:
Why?? It looks real! There's even a timer on the page.

She had already clicked the link.

It opened a page that *looked* like Instagram — same colors, same font, same layout — asking her to log in to verify her account.

She typed her username and password quickly, eager to claim her "prize."
The page blinked. Then crashed.

Riya (confused):
Um... weird. Did it work?

 10 Minutes Later...

Riya was suddenly logged out of Instagram.

Then her WhatsApp pinged.

Aman:
"Dude, are you DMing random people asking for money?"

Aaliya (classmate):
"Riya?? What's this weird message about UPI and emergencies?"

She tried logging back in. Her password wasn't working.

Her Instagram had been hijacked.

 Panic Mode

Riya ran to her dad.

Riya:
"Papa... I think I clicked a wrong link."

Dad:
"Start from the beginning. What happened?"

She explained the giveaway. The login page. The messages.

Her father helped her report the account to Instagram and change her email password. Thankfully, she had 2-step verification on her email. That helped her recover access before the hacker could lock her out completely.

❓ What Just Happened?

Riya fell for a phishing scam — a fake login page that steals your username and password when you type it in. These pages:

- Look exactly like real apps (Instagram, Facebook, etc.)
- Often use slightly misspelled URLs or fake domains
- Promise exciting prizes or make urgent requests
- Hijack your account and send the same message to your friends, spreading the scam

---

📚 LESSON: Think Before You Click

1. Even "Real" Looking Links Can Be Fake

- Check the URL carefully.
  instagift-prize.win/ig-login is NOT the same as instagram.com
- Scam pages mimic login screens — they don't actually verify anything.

2. If They Ask You to Log In, Pause

Always ask:

- Who is sending this?
- Why would they need my password?
- Does the page have HTTPS (secure connection)?

3. Turn On Two-Factor Authentication

If someone gets your password, 2FA can stop them.
Use apps like:

- Google Authenticator
- Microsoft Authenticator
- Instagram's built-in 2FA settings

☑ If This Happens to You:

1. Change your password immediately
   Log out of all other devices
2. Report the scam account to the platform
3. Tell your friends not to click anything forwarded from you
4. Turn on 2FA to prevent future attacks

 Final Thought:

One click. That's all it takes.

Scammers don't need to break passwords — they just need you to give it to them willingly.

So next time you see a "Congrats! You've won" message...

> Don't rush. Don't type. Don't click.
> Just pause — and protect yourself.

REMEMBER:

Phishing Comes in Many Forms — Not Just Instagram Links

Phishing isn't just about flashy giveaway messages on social media.
Scammers use emails, SMS, websites, and even phone calls to trick you into giving away:

- Passwords
- OTPs
- Personal details
- Bank information

Here are the most common types — with examples you might recognize:

---

1. Email Phishing

Looks like: An official-looking email from a bank, school, or popular service like Google or Netflix.

Subject line:

> *"URGENT: Your Account Has Been Suspended. Verify Now."*

Message:

> "Dear user, we noticed suspicious activity on your Gmail account. Please verify your identity within 24 hours or your account will be locked. Click here to login: secure-login-g00gle.com"

What's happening?

- The link goes to a fake login page
- As soon as you enter your password, it's stolen
- You may be redirected to the real site so you don't notice anything went wrong

☑ How to spot it:

- The sender's email looks strange: secure@g00gle-account-alerts.xyz
- It uses urgency: *"last warning"*, *"account locked"*
- The link is not the official domain

2. Smishing (SMS Phishing)

Looks like: A text message from your bank, delivery service, or UPI provider

Message:

> "Your SBI account has been frozen due to suspicious activity. Click here to unblock: sbi-verify-login.info"
> Or: "Your parcel is held. Pay ₹50 to release delivery: courier-pay.in"

What's happening?

- You're tricked into entering card or UPI info
- Or they install spyware via a downloaded app

☑ How to spot it:

- Banks don't send clickable links via SMS
- Courier companies won't ask for money through random links
- Always check sender ID and URL carefully

3. Vishing (Voice Phishing)

Looks like: A phone call from someone pretending to be from a bank, government agency, or delivery service.

Example:

"Hello, sir. I'm calling from your bank. There's a problem with your KYC. If you don't complete it now, your account will be frozen. Please share your Aadhaar and OTP."

What's happening?

- They use fear to make you act fast
- They may even have some personal info to sound "real"
- Once you give OTP or UPI PIN — your money is gone

☑ How to spot it:

- Banks never ask for OTP, PIN, or CVV on calls
- Real agencies never threaten to freeze accounts over the phone
- Always hang up and call the bank directly

4. Fake App or Login Page Phishing

Looks like: A fake version of a real site or app

Example:

- You search for "IRCTC login" on Google
- Click the first link (a fake ad)
- Enter your username and password
- Your account is compromised

☑ How to stay safe:

- Always type official URLs directly (irctc.co.in, not random links)
- Download apps only from official app stores

📢 Final Takeaway for Readers:

Phishing is like a digital costume party. Everything *looks* official — but it's all an act.

> Before you click a link, share your info, or respond to a message...
> Ask yourself: Would this company/person really contact me this way?

🧠 Remember:

When in doubt, don't click. Don't type. Don't talk.
Just stop — and verify.

---

6. Digital Robin Hood: Ponzi Scam

<u>"How a Promised Profit Turned Into a Vanished Dream"</u>

Characters:

- *Ritika* – 16, studious, curious, careful
- *Parag* – Ritika's classmate, outgoing and always on the hunt for the next "cool" thing
- *Ritika's Dad* – works in banking, appears later

[Scene: After school, at a café. Parag is showing something on his phone.]

Parag (excited):
 Ritika, look! I made ₹1,500 in just two days using this new app — Fxtrading Pro. You just invest a little, and it doubles super fast.

Ritika (raising an eyebrow):
 Seriously? That sounds fake.

Parag:
 It's not! My cousin uses it too. You just deposit ₹1,000, and they "auto-invest" it in crypto and forex or something. I've already withdrawn money once. Look — here's the screenshot.

[Ritika sees a sleek app interface, with earnings going up in real time.]

Ritika:
Hmm... It looks real. But... who are these people running it?

Parag:
Who cares? It works. I'm going to put in ₹5,000 next week. You should try with ₹500. Come on — everyone in our tuition group is doing it.

[Later that night at home...]

Ritika (to her dad):
Papa, have you heard of an app called Fxtrading Pro? Some of my friends are investing in it. They're getting returns in 48 hours...

Dad (instantly alert):
Fxtrading Pro? That sounds like a Ponzi scheme. These apps pay old users with new users' money — and then vanish overnight. One of my colleagues' daughters lost ₹80,000 in something just like that.

Ritika:
But Parag showed me screenshots!

Dad:
That's how they hook you. First payout is real. Second one might be. By the third, you've added more money — and *poof*, the app disappears.

[Next week: the app stops working. Parag panics. So do others.]

Parag (messaging frantically):
  Ritika, the app is down! My ₹5,000 is stuck! No one's replying!

? What Just Happened?

Ritika made the smart choice — she paused and asked questions. Parag didn't. He fell for a modern Ponzi scheme, disguised as a sleek investment app. These scams reward early users to build trust, then crash the system and disappear with everyone's money.

They often spread through social groups, where pressure and excitement make people act fast — and think less.

Real Example

Dipankar Barman, the owner of DB Stock, ran a fake trading and investment network that operated as a Ponzi scheme in Assam. He promised high daily returns in the name of stock market trading, but there was no real trading involved.

Many people, including students and small-town families, invested lakhs — even crores — of rupees, lured by fake profit screenshots and fast withdrawals.

When the money stopped coming in, Dipankar disappeared, and the Telegram groups were deleted. By the time people realized the truth, it was too late — the money was gone, and hundreds of lives were affected.

This case is a strong reminder:

> If someone guarantees profits from trading — without risk, licenses, or official channels — it's not investment. It's a trap.

 ## Lesson: How to Spot Fake Investment Traps

1. High Returns + No Risk = SCAM

No real investment doubles your money overnight. If an app promises huge rewards with "no loss," it's not an opportunity — it's bait.

2. Scams Spread Through Friends Too

Just because a classmate or cousin is using something doesn't make it safe. They may not even know it's a scam until it's too late.

3. Professional Look Doesn't Mean It's Legit

Scam apps use great design, logos, fake certificates and fake reviews. Always check the company name, reviews on trusted platforms, and if it's listed on official app stores.

4. Ask These 3 Questions Before You Invest:

- Who runs it? (Are they registered, traceable?)

- Where is the money actually going?
- Can you verify the company online through government or bank sources?

5. Talk to Someone Who Understands Finance

Even ₹500 matters. If you're not sure, ask a teacher, parent, or someone who works in banking or finance.

☑ Signs of a Ponzi Scheme (Fake Investment App):

- You get paid only when you bring new users
- They urge you to "level up" by investing more
- The company has no real address or customer support
- There's no license, regulation, or proof of actual trading

Remember: Peer pressure can make even smart students fall for scams.

The best investment you can make right now?
Increase your own awareness.

---

7. The Stolen Identity

(What If Someone Pretended to Be You?)

Characters:

- *Ananya* – 15, active on Instagram and school group chats
- *Sneha* – her friend who first spots the fake profile
- *"Ananya Singh Official"* – the impersonator account
- *Ananya's Teacher* – offers support and action steps

[Scene: Ananya is heading to class when Sneha runs up to her, holding her phone.]

Sneha (worried):
 Ananya, did you create a second Instagram account? Like a backup or something?

Ananya:
 Huh? No… why?

Sneha:
 There's a profile called "*@ananya_singh_official_*" — it has your profile pic and even your bio. But it's following random boys and messaging weird stuff.

Ananya (shocked):
 Wait… WHAT!?

[They open the account. Same photo, same name, same school in bio. But the posts are odd. The messages are flirty and awkward.]

Ananya:
 This isn't me! Someone's pretending to be me. This is so creepy.

Sneha:
 Should we report it?

Ananya (panicking):
 What if people think it *is* me? What if teachers see it?

[Later that day, Ananya gathers courage and talks to her class teacher after school.]

Ananya:
 Ma'am… I think someone made a fake profile using my name and photos. They're messaging people. I didn't do it.

Teacher (calmly):
 You did the right thing by telling me. This is called identity theft, and it's serious — but it's not your fault. We'll report the account together and inform your parents. You are not in trouble.

Ananya (relieved):
 Thank you, ma'am. I just didn't want anyone to believe I was behind it.

[The school helps her report the account. Her friends also report it, and Instagram removes it within a day. Ananya posts a story from her real account clarifying the situation.]

❓ What Just Happened?

Ananya was the victim of online impersonation, also known as catfishing — when someone creates a fake account using your name, photo, and personal info to trick others.

Scammers and bullies do this to:

- Spread lies or fake messages
- Harass or prank classmates
- Ruin someone's reputation
- Manipulate or scam others using their identity

📚 Lesson: What to Do If Someone Pretends to Be You Online

1. Don't Panic — It's Not Your Fault

You didn't do anything wrong. The person copying you is the one at fault.
 Stay calm and take action.

2. Take Screenshots

Save proof of the fake account:

- Username
- Posts and messages
- Followers
  You'll need this to report it properly.

3. Report the Profile (and Ask Friends to Do the Same)

Most social apps let you:

- Report the account as impersonation
- Block the account
- Submit identity proof if needed (Instagram/FB sometimes ask)

The more people who report, the faster the action.

4. Tell a Trusted Adult Immediately

Talk to:
- A parent
- Teacher or school counselor
- Older sibling

They can help file a proper complaint and support you emotionally.

5. Secure Your Real Account

- Make it private
- Remove personal details from your bio
- Use a unique profile picture not used elsewhere
- Turn on two-factor authentication (2FA)

☑ Signs of a Fake Profile:

- Same name + photos, but a slightly altered username
- Messages sent that don't sound like you
- Sudden follows or chats with strangers
- Bio that sounds off or overly dramatic

🧠 Remember:

Your identity belongs to you — and no one has the right to use your face, name, or voice without your consent.

If someone tries to fake your presence online...
 don't hide — take charge.

Because the real you is powerful, confident, and protected — not just by privacy settings, but by knowledge.

🔍 Other Real-World Dangers of Identity Theft

Once someone has your name, photo, Aadhaar, PAN, or even your phone number, they can do serious damage.

Here's how:

1. Buying a SIM Card in Your Name

- Using your ID proof, scammers can get a duplicate SIM
- They hijack your number and:
  - Steal OTPs

- Take over your WhatsApp or bank account
- Use your number in scams

2. Taking Loans or Credit Cards Using Your PAN

- Fraudsters apply for instant loans in your name
- You may not know until:
  - Collection agents start calling
  - Your credit score crashes

3. Opening Bank Accounts to Launder Money

- Scammers use fake KYC documents to open illegal accounts
- These accounts are used to:
  - Move scam money
  - Fund criminal activity

4. Using Your Identity to Commit Cybercrimes

- Fake accounts in your name may:
  - Harass others
  - Ask for money from your friends
  - Send inappropriate messages

You could be blamed if they don't know it's fake.

5. Romance or Matrimony Scams

- Fake profiles on dating or marriage apps using your name/photo
- Used to trap people emotionally — or financially

6. Using Your Documents to Apply for Jobs or Exams

- Mark sheets, Aadhaar, or certificates misused for:
    - Government jobs
    - School/college admissions
    - Fake resumes

7. Getting Targeted Again

Once you're hit once, your details might be:

- Sold on the dark web
- Used in future scams
- Shared with other criminals

 LESSON: How to Stay Safe from Identity Theft

1. Never Share Full Documents Publicly

- Don't post your ID, admit cards, or certificates online
- If you need to upload, add a watermark like *"For school use only"*
- Use pins and authentications. <u>Lock your aadhar</u> and only share masked aadhar if required.

2. Use 2-Factor Authentication

- On all important apps: Instagram, Gmail, banking
- Use authenticator apps instead of just phone numbers

3. Monitor Your Accounts

- Check bank statements and credit reports

- Log out of unknown devices on Google/Meta

4. Report Fake Profiles or Activity Immediately

- On Instagram: Use "Report > Impersonation"
- File a complaint. (Check chapter 19)

5. Tell Someone. Don't Stay Silent

- Talk to a parent, teacher, or counselor
- You're not in trouble — you're the victim

8. The Online Job Scam

<u>(When Students Protect Their Family)</u>

Characters:

- *Ishaan* – 14, alert, reads about online frauds
- *Uncle Rajesh* – Ishaan's mama (mother's brother), recently lost his job
- *"QuickTask India"* – the fake job provider
- *Ishaan's Mom* – appears later

[Scene: Sunday afternoon. Ishaan walks into the living room where his uncle Rajesh is filling a form on his phone, looking hopeful.]

Ishaan:
 Mama, what are you doing?

Uncle Rajesh:
 Applying for a remote data entry job. Found it on a Telegram group. They're offering ₹3,000 per day — just entering survey data.

Ishaan (curious):
 Sounds good... what's the company name?

Uncle Rajesh:
 "QuickTask India." No interviews, no experience needed.

Just fill this Google Form and pay a ₹599 "registration" fee.

Ishaan (eyes widening):
 Wait... pay to get a job?

[Ishaan sits down beside him and opens his own phone.]

Ishaan:
 Mama, can I check that website?

[They go to the site. It's flashy but has no About page, no company address, and weird grammar.]

Ishaan:
 Mama... this is fake. See? No real contact details, no LinkedIn, and they're asking hundreds of people to "register" by sending money through UPI.

Uncle Rajesh (uncertain):
 But it was shared by someone in our colony group. And a lady there said she got her first salary.

Ishaan:
 Scammers often fake testimonials. They even send "first payments" to build trust, and then vanish after bigger payments.

[Ishaan's mom enters.]

Ishaan's Mom:
 What's going on?

Ishaan:
 Mama almost paid for a fake job. They're running a classic scam — promise work, ask for a small payment, and then disappear.

Mom (firmly):
 Good you caught it. Rajesh, from now on, if anything sounds too good to be true, ask Ishaan first. He's better at spotting scams than most adults!

[Uncle Rajesh laughs, slightly embarrassed but thankful.]

Uncle Rajesh:
 Thanks, beta. I didn't know students knew this stuff better than us now!

❓ What Just Happened?

Uncle Rajesh nearly fell for an online job scam, a common fraud where fake companies offer easy, high-paying remote jobs — but only after a "processing" or "registration" fee is paid.

The job never exists. The moment enough people pay, the scammer:

- Disappears
- Blocks everyone

- Starts again under a new name

These scams target unemployed adults, homemakers, and seniors, who may not know how real online jobs work.

📚 Lesson: Spotting Online Job Scams (And Helping Your Family)

1. Real Jobs Don't Ask You to Pay First

No legit employer will ask you to:

- Pay to register
- Buy software or "kits"
- Send money to a recruiter via UPI

If you're paying to work — it's a scam.

2. Check for These Red Flags

- Telegram/WhatsApp-only communication
- No company website or physical address
- No interview or real HR interaction
- Very generic job title: "Online Worker", "Survey Entry", "Easy Money Job"

3. Too Good to Be True = Too Good to Be Real

₹3,000 per day for data entry? No experience? No skills? Scammers know this sounds tempting — especially when someone needs money. That's why they use it.

4. As a Student, You Can Help Adults Stay Safe

Many parents or uncles/aunts may not spot online fraud —
but you can.
 Help them:

- Google the company name
- Check for reviews or warnings
- Look up scam reports on YouTube or forums

5. What to Do If Someone Fell for It

- Note the UPI ID and report it. (Check chapter 19).
- Share the scam in your local WhatsApp group to prevent others.
- Talk to someone — it's okay to feel embarrassed, but better to learn and move on.

🧠 Remember:
 Scammers don't just target kids — they exploit your family's hope and need.
 Your knowledge can protect them.

Be the digital shield your family needs.

---

9. Deepfake Danger

<u>(Don't Believe Everything You See — Literally)</u>

Characters:

- *Zara* – 14, active on YouTube and social media
- *Mitali* – her best friend, creative and cautious
- A *"Blackmailer"* – anonymous scammer using fake video
- *Zara's Cousin (Rohit)* – studying cybersecurity

[Scene: Zara opens her phone to find an anonymous message on Instagram from a private account called "@truth_exposed_real."]

Message:
 "We have a video of you doing something embarrassing. If you don't want this sent to your friends, pay ₹3,000 via UPI. You have 3 hours."
 [Attached: A blurry video where someone who looks like Zara appears to be saying something inappropriate.]

Zara (gasps):
 What the—!? That's not me! But... it *looks* like me. My face, my voice?

[She rushes to Mitali at lunch break, looking shaken.]

Zara:
 Mitu... someone sent me a video. It looks like I'm saying gross stuff — but I swear I didn't! They're blackmailing me.

Mitali (calmly):
 Show me. Don't panic yet.

[They watch the video together. It looks real, but Zara's voice sounds slightly robotic. The background is generic. No clear context.]

Mitali:
 Zara... I've read about this. I think this is a deepfake. AI can now fake faces and voices using just a few photos or clips from your posts.

Zara:
 So... they can make me say anything!?

Mitali:
 Yes. And they use that to scare you into sending money.

[Later that day, they call Zara's cousin Rohit, a cybersecurity student.]

Rohit (on call):
 This is happening a lot now. They use AI tools to create fake videos — especially of girls. It's emotional blackmail. Don't respond, don't pay, and don't stay silent.

Zara:

But what if others think it's real?

Rohit:

That's why you report it immediately. Most platforms take these threats seriously now. And the faster you act, the safer you stay.

[Zara reports the account, blocks the sender, and informs her school counselor. Her parents support her — and nothing further happens. The scammer moves on, but she stands her ground.]

❓ What Just Happened?

Zara faced a deepfake scam — a new form of cyber threat where scammers use AI to create fake videos, voices, or images to manipulate and blackmail students.

They often:

- Steal selfies or videos from social media
- Use free AI tools to generate realistic fakes
- Threaten to send them to friends/family unless paid
- Target girls more often, using shame or fear as leverage

 Lesson: How to Handle Deepfake Threats

1. Pause. Don't Panic.

Even if the video looks real — it might not be. Deepfakes are made to trigger emotion before logic.

> If it feels sudden, scary, and demanding — take a deep breath.

2. Watch for Clues

- Voice doesn't match tone or personality
- Blurry or mismatched facial movements
- No specific details — just general threats
- Often sent from new or anonymous accounts

3. Never Pay or Respond

Paying doesn't make the problem go away — it only encourages the scammer. They may come back asking for more.

4. Block, Report, and Tell Someone Immediately:

- Block the sender
- Report the message or video (on Instagram, WhatsApp, etc
- Talk to a parent, counselor, or teacher

You don't need to face this alone.
 Cyberbullying or blackmail is a crime, not your shame.

5. Protect Your Photos and Videos

- Keep your accounts private
- Avoid sharing close-up selfies or videos publicly
- Be mindful of what you post — especially if your face and voice are visible

---

☑ Signs You're Dealing With a Deepfake Scam:

- The person claims to have a "video" but won't prove it fully
- They use scare tactics: "Pay or I'll leak this"
- They contact you from a strange account, then disappear
- They act fast and push emotional buttons: fear, shame, urgency
- Deepfakes can also be used for Impersonating Authorities or Celebrities, voice cloning or manipulation scams.

Remember:

Technology can fake faces — but truth is still stronger.
If you didn't do it, don't be afraid of it.

Stand tall. Tell someone.
Because the best way to beat a digital lie... is with real support.

---

10. The Homework Helper Trap

<u>(When 'Free Help' Isn't Really Free)</u>

Characters:

- *Yashvi* – 14, smart, but rushing through schoolwork
- *Priya* – her best friend, cautious and curious
- *"EduMaster AI"* – the suspicious app
- *Yashvi's Elder Brother (Ishan)* – tech-savvy college student

---

[Scene: Yashvi is working on a history worksheet at home, bored and frustrated.]

Yashvi (groaning):
  Ugh! How am I supposed to write 150 words on the Mughal administration by *tomorrow morning*?

[She opens YouTube and searches: "AI app to solve homework." A video pops up titled "Top 3 Apps That Do Homework FOR YOU 📢"]

YouTuber:
  Download EduMaster AI — just upload a pic of the question and boom! Instant answer. Free. No ads. No login needed.

[Yashvi clicks the link in the description. It leads to a third-party website. She downloads the APK file and installs the app.]

App:
 Allow access to camera, storage, SMS, contacts, and microphone?

Yashvi (muttering):
 Why does it need SMS? Whatever. Allow.

[Next day at school...]

Priya:
 Yash, you finished the worksheet?

Yashvi:
 Done. AI magic. Just snapped a photo — got a whole paragraph back in seconds. No thinking needed

Priya:
 Wait... which app?

Yashvi:
 Something called EduMaster AI. I found it on YouTube.

Priya (frowning):
 That's not on Play Store. You sure it's safe?

Yashvi:
 It works fine. Who cares?

[Later that evening...]

Yashvi's phone starts acting weird. Pop-up ads on the lock screen. Battery drains. She receives a message saying: "Thank you for registering for EduSubscription — ₹599 will be charged."]

Yashvi (panicked):
 WHAT?! I didn't subscribe to anything!

[Her brother, Ishan, walks in.]

Yashvi:
 Bhaiya, my phone's acting crazy! And now it says I paid for something I didn't even buy!

Ishan (checking):
 You downloaded an APK from a shady website? And gave it SMS permission?

Yashvi:
 I... just wanted help with history 

Ishan (seriously):
 Yashvi, that app was probably spyware. It may have auto-subscribed you using silent SMS commands. Worse — it could be reading your messages or even listening through the mic.

 # What Just Happened?

Yashvi was tricked by a fake "AI homework" app — one that seemed helpful, but actually collected her data and may have triggered unauthorized payments or injected adware/malware.

These apps look useful on the surface but exploit permissions, send private info to servers, and sometimes control parts of your phone in the background.

 ## Lesson: How to Stay Smart with "Study Tools"

1. Only Use Apps from Trusted Stores

If it's not on Google Play Store or Apple App Store, it hasn't been verified. Avoid downloading ".apk" files from websites or YouTube links.

2. Never Allow All Permissions Blindly

If a study app asks for:

- SMS
- Contacts
- Microphone
- Call logs

  That's not normal. Click "Deny." Uninstall immediately.

3. Real Learning ≠ Copy-Paste

AI can help you understand — but not replace your learning. Apps that do the work *for you* often come with a price: your privacy.

4. Be Wary of Auto-Subscriptions or SMS Charges

Scam apps can sign you up for paid services silently, especially if SMS and call permissions are enabled. Always check your SMS inbox and wallet apps.

5. Talk to an Adult or Senior If You Suspect Something

It's okay to be curious. But if something feels "off" — slow phone, unknown messages, weird behavior — ask someone for help. Better to be safe than sorry.

11. Love, Lies & Matrimony Scams

(A Brother's Lesson to Protect His Sister)

Characters:

- *Anuj* – 15, observant, reads about online scams, protective of his sister
- *Nisha Didi* – 23, kind, romantic, recently joined a matrimony platform
- *"Raj"* – an NRI groom… or so he claims
- *Their Mom* – appears briefly

[Scene: Nisha is sitting on the sofa, smiling at her phone. Anuj walks in with a plate of snacks.]

Anuj:
 Didi, why are you grinning like that? New meme or full marks in love life?

Nisha (laughs):
 Shut up, silly. Just chatting with someone. His name's Raj — he messaged me on a matrimony site.

Anuj (sits beside her):
 Ohhh. Raj? Sounds fancy. What's his story?

Nisha:
 He says he's working in London — software engineer.

Super polite, family-oriented. He wants to settle down in India and says I seem "different from other girls."

Anuj (raising an eyebrow):
 Wow, that's quick. When did you two start chatting?

Nisha:
 Like, three days ago... but we've talked a lot. He already calls me "his person." Cute, no?

Anuj (gently):
 Didi... don't you think it's a little *too* much, too fast?

Nisha:
 He's just expressive. He even said he's planning to visit India next month — and wants to meet us.

Anuj:
 Did he ask for anything yet?

Nisha (pauses):
 Well... he said his UK bank account is having issues and asked if he could temporarily send some money to my account, just until he arrives.

Anuj (serious now):
 Didi. That's the scam. This sounds exactly like a matrimony scam I read about. They talk sweet, build trust fast, say they're NRIs, and then ask for favors like money transfers, parcel clearance fees, or visa help.

Nisha (confused):
 But he hasn't asked *me* for money. Just to hold his for a bit.

Anuj:
 It starts there. Next, he'll say his "courier got stuck" or he needs a quick "processing fee" paid to someone. And if you send it, he'll vanish.

[He grabs his tablet, types in "matrimony fraud NRI India" and shows her multiple articles about women scammed the exact same way.]

Anuj:
 These are real stories. Smart women, just like you, who believed the guy — until they lost thousands. Some even took loans. And none of those "Raj"s ever existed.

[Later, Nisha tells their mom and blocks the account. She's embarrassed, but thankful.]

Nisha:
 Anuj, I honestly didn't think someone could fake all that... he was so convincing.

Anuj:
 That's what they do, Di. It's not about being silly — they study people's emotions and use that trust against them.

❓ What Just Happened?

Nisha was being targeted in a love/matrimony scam — a rising fraud in India where scammers pretend to be well-settled NRIs or romantic partners, then use emotional manipulation to gain trust... and eventually, money.

They use:

- Compliments and affection early on
- Emotional bonding: "You're special," "I've never felt this before"
- Fake problems: stuck parcels, blocked accounts, visa issues
- Guilt or urgency: "Help me, don't you trust me?"

📚 Lesson: Spotting a Matrimony or Romance Scam (And Helping Your Family Do the Same)

1. Too Much, Too Soon Is a Warning Sign

If someone expresses love, attachment, or commitment within days — pause. Real relationships take time. Scams are always fast.

2. Foreign Location + Money Talk = RED FLAG

Scammers often say they're from:

- UK, Canada, Dubai, Australia
  Then create believable problems like:
- "Courier stuck in customs"
- "Bank account frozen"
- "Stuck at the airport and need help with visa/legal fee"

3. They Sound Perfect... Because They're Not Real

Scammers study profiles and say what the victim wants to hear:

- "Family values"
- "Tired of fake people"
- "I want something real"

  They're not looking for love — they're looking for access.

4. Educate Your Sisters, Cousins & Moms

Women of all ages — especially those on matrimony sites — need to know how this scam works. As a student, you can be the one who helps them see the signs.

5. Never Share Bank Details or Accept Money Transfers

Even if they promise "it's just temporary." If it's illegal money, you could get in legal trouble too.

☑ Signs of a Love/Matrimony Scam:

- Over-affectionate too quickly
- Says "don't tell anyone"
- Keeps chatting on WhatsApp instead of video calling
- Tries to isolate you emotionally
- Introduces a money-related issue after building trust

Remember:

Online love can feel real — but emotions are the easiest thing to fake.

Help the women in your life stay alert.
Being a digital defender isn't just about your safety —
It's about protecting the people you love, too.

---

12. Groomed by Trust

How Online Strangers Target Girls

Characters:

- *Ishita* – 14, bright, creative, loves poetry and photography
- *"Rahul"* – an online friend who seems perfect
- *Riya* – Ishita's elder cousin, college student
- *Ishita's Mom* – appears later

[Scene: Evening. Ishita is browsing an online writing group on Instagram where people share poems, thoughts, and art.]

[She receives a comment on her poem post:]

_rahul_writer98:
Beautiful lines. You write with a lot of depth. Are you in 11th? You seem mature for your age.

[Later, a DM appears.]

Rahul:
Hey Ishita, hope you don't mind me messaging. Your poetry really stood out to me. I'm a writer too — would love to exchange thoughts.

Ishita (typing):
 Thanks! That means a lot. Most people just like and scroll

[Over the next few weeks, they chat regularly. Rahul is polite, funny, compliments her often, asks about her day.]

Rahul:
 You're really different from others I talk to. You actually listen. I feel like I can tell you anything.

Ishita:
 Haha, you're easy to talk to. What do you write?

Rahul:
 Mostly late-night thoughts. Wanna read one I haven't shared with anyone else?

[One evening...]

Rahul:
 You know, I've never had someone understand me like this. Do you have a recent photo of yourself? I just want to see the person behind the words. I'll send mine too.

Ishita (hesitant):
 Umm... I don't usually share pics.

Rahul:
 No pressure. It's just... I feel close to you, and it would mean a lot.

[Later, she tells her cousin Riya.]

Ishita:

Di, there's this guy I met through my poetry page. He's sweet. We talk a lot. He sent me a photo and wants mine now.

Riya (stops scrolling):

How long have you known him?

Ishita:

A few weeks... he says he's 17. Lives in Pune.

Riya:

Ishita, I need to tell you something important. This is exactly how online grooming begins. It may feel real — but you don't actually know him. He could be lying about everything.

Ishita (confused):

But he's been kind. He talks like someone who really cares.

Riya:

That's part of the trap. They build trust, give compliments, make you feel special — and then start asking for photos, secrets, or even meetups. Please don't send anything. You need to tell Mom.

[Ishita, still shaken but thankful, talks to her mom with Riya by her side. Together, they report and block Rahul's account.]

❓ What Just Happened?

Ishita was being groomed online — a process where a stranger slowly builds trust through kind words, emotional connection, and patience... all with the intention to exploit.

Online grooming doesn't start with threats. It starts with:

- "You're special."
- "No one understands me like you."
- "Don't tell anyone about our chats."

And then it moves to:

- "Send me a photo."
- "Let's meet."
- "You can trust me. Others won't understand."

📚 Lesson: How to Spot and Stop Online Grooming

<u>1. They Build an Emotional Connection First</u>

Groomers don't rush. They spend days or weeks making you feel seen, heard, and valued. That's how they earn your trust.

2. Then They Start Asking for "Just One" Photo or Secret

Even if it feels small, it's not. A simple selfie can be misused. And once they have something, they may pressure or blackmail you.

3. Real Friends Don't Push Boundaries

If someone keeps asking for something you're not comfortable with — even after you say no — they're not a friend. That's manipulation.

4. You're Not "Overreacting" for Being Cautious

It's okay to block, report, or say no — even if the person *seems nice*. Your gut is smarter than you think.

5. Always Talk to Someone You Trust

If someone makes you feel uncomfortable, confused, or pressured — tell a cousin, teacher, parent, or school counselor. You won't get in trouble. You'll get help.

☑ Red Flags of Grooming:

- They message you privately after seeing a public post
- They compliment you *too much, too soon*

- They ask for photos or emotional secrets early on
- They want to move chats to private apps like Telegram or Snapchat
- They say things like "don't tell anyone" or "others won't understand us"

🧠 Remember:

It's okay to share your art, your voice, your ideas.

But your body, your face, your personal world? That's yours alone.

If someone tries to earn your trust just to cross your boundaries —

That's not friendship. That's manipulation.

Be kind. Be confident. But above all, be safe.

---

13. When Cyberbullying Gets Real

<u>"Words Hurt. Screens Don't Protect."</u>

Characters:

- *Simran* – 15, kind, sensitive, shares everything with her best friend
- *Neha* – Simran's friend... until things change
- *Tanya* – their classmate, quiet but observant
- *Simran's Teacher* – appears briefly, supportive

[Scene: School corridor, break time. Simran and Neha are leaning against the wall, laughing over memes.]

Neha:

You know what would be hilarious? If I post that photo of you trying to dance at last year's farewell. Remember how you tripped?

Simran (laughing):

Nooo! That was so embarrassing! Don't even think about it.

Neha:

Relax, I'm just kidding. I still have access to your Instagram anyway. You gave me the password during board prep, remember?

Simran (pauses):
 Yeah… I forgot to change it. You didn't check my DMs, right?

Neha (smirking):
Why? Hiding something? 

[Later that week, Simran notices something strange. Her old, embarrassing photos appear in a group chat. People are laughing. Tanya walks up to her in class.]

Tanya:
 Hey… just so you know, Neha posted some screenshots of your chats in the "Fun School" WhatsApp group. You might want to check.

Simran (shocked):
 What!? Why would she—!?

[Simran opens her phone. Her stomach drops. Neha had used her account to share private DMs and photos — as a "joke." The group was mocking her. She feels humiliated.]

Simran (texting Neha):
 How could you do this? You knew I trusted you!

Neha (cold reply):
 Chill, it was just for fun. Stop being dramatic.

[Simran spends the day quiet, withdrawn. After class, she walks up to her teacher.]

Simran (softly):
  Ma'am... if someone shares something personal online, without permission... what can you do?

Teacher:
  You come to me with details. Right now. This is cyberbullying, Simran — and it's never "just for fun." We'll make sure it stops.

❓ What Just Happened?

Simran was cyberbullied by someone she trusted. By sharing her password, she gave Neha control over her private account — and that trust was broken.

What started as a friendship turned into humiliation. This is how digital consent works — your photos, messages, and identity belong to you. No one has the right to use them, even "as a joke."

Lesson: Passwords, Privacy & Protecting Yourself

1. Never Share Passwords — Even With Friends

Friendships can change. Trust doesn't mean giving access to your entire online life. Keep your passwords private — always.

2. Digital Consent Is Real Consent

Just like in real life, no one can post your pictures, chats, or personal info without permission.

NO means NO — even online.

3. "Just Joking" Isn't a Defense

When someone causes emotional harm, even if they say "it was a joke," it's still bullying. Your feelings matter.

4. Don't Suffer in Silence

If you're being harassed or humiliated online:

- Take screenshots
- Block the bully
- Report the account
- Talk to an adult: teacher, counselor, or parent

5. Change Passwords Immediately If Shared

If someone else has your login info, update your password and turn on two-factor authentication (2FA). That way, even they can't log in again.

☑ Signs You're Being Cyberbullied:

- People post about you in group chats or anonymously
- You feel nervous or anxious opening your phone
- Friends laugh at something you didn't know was shared
- Someone uses your private info to embarrass you
- The person says "you're too sensitive" instead of apologizing

Remember:

Your digital self is still *you*.

You deserve privacy, respect, and protection — online and offline.

If someone crosses a line, speak up.
You're not being "dramatic."
You're being brave.

14. The Scammer in Uniform

<u>"When Fake Authority Meets Real Fear"</u>

Characters:

- *Rohit* – 17, disciplined student, tech-smart but sometimes anxious
- *Kunal* – Rohit's friend, a bit more chill and skeptical
- *Rohit's Mom* – appears later

[Scene: Rohit is alone at home on a Saturday afternoon. He gets a call from a number labeled "Mumbai Cyber Cell" — though he lives in Lucknow.]

Caller (firm voice):
 Is this Rohit Sharma?

Rohit:
 Yes... speaking.

Caller:
 This is Inspector Anil Yadav from the Mumbai Cyber Crime Branch. Your Aadhaar number has been found linked to a money laundering case.

Rohit (nervously):
 W-what? That's not possible! What money laundering?

Caller (serious):
 A parcel registered under your name was intercepted in Mumbai. It contained cash and documents connected to illegal activity. You may be involved — knowingly or unknowingly.

Rohit:
 This has to be a mistake. I didn't send any parcel!

Caller:
 You can explain yourself. But first, we need to verify your identity. And this call is being recorded for legal purposes. If you disconnect or fail to cooperate, we will have to escalate the case and issue a digital warrant.

[Rohit's heart starts racing. He's sweating, pacing.]

[Just then, Kunal texts him.]

Kunal (chat):
 Bro, you coming to practice?

Rohit (typing fast):
 Dude, I'm on a call with cyber police. They said my Aadhaar is in a crime case. I'm in BIG trouble.

Kunal:
 Wait WHAT? Real police?

Rohit:
 Yes! They have documents, they sound serious, and they said if I hang up, they'll issue a warrant!

Kunal:

That sounds weird, man. Police don't call like that. Don't panic. Did they ask for any details?

Rohit:

Just bank account and Aadhaar confirmation so far. They said they'll "temporarily freeze" my account to check for illegal money.

Kunal:

ROHIT. That's a SCAM. Hang up and tell your mom NOW.

[Rohit hesitates... then ends the call. Walks straight to his mom.]

Rohit (shaken):

Maa, I think someone tried to scam me. They sounded like police... said I was in trouble... I almost gave them my account details.

Mom (hugging him):

It's okay, beta. You didn't do anything wrong. But yes — that was a scam. I've read about it. People lose lakhs like this.

❓ What Just Happened?

Rohit experienced a "fake police scam" — a growing type of fraud where scammers impersonate police officers or government officials. Their strategy? Scare the victim, isolate them, and pressure them to hand over personal or financial details.

They often use real-sounding titles, official logos, and urgent language like:

- "This is a serious legal matter."
- "Don't tell anyone, this is a confidential investigation."
- "You must cooperate or face arrest."

📌 Real Example: The Hyderabad FedEx Fraud (2024)

An 85-year-old man from Hyderabad received an alarming call from a customs official claiming that a parcel in his name had been intercepted by authorities, linking him to illegal activities. Panicked, he believed the callers, who posed as officials from FedEx, customs, and law enforcement agencies. Over the course of several days, these fraudsters skillfully manipulated him into transferring a staggering ₹2.88 crore to various bank accounts.

But the truth?

There was no parcel. No illegal activity.

The callers weren't officials; they were scammers who exploited fear and trust. The elderly victim, innocent and unsuspecting, was defrauded simply because he trusted the misinformation he received over a phone call.

 Lesson: How to Spot Fake Legal Threat Scams

1. Real Police Never Demand Personal Info Over the Phone

No real cop or government officer will call and ask for your bank details, Aadhaar number, or OTP — especially not for a crime you've never heard of.

2. "Digital Warrant" Is Not a Real Thing

Scammers invent fancy-sounding phrases like "digital arrest," "CBI surveillance," or "RBI freeze" to sound serious. These are scare tactics — not real procedures.

3. Fear Blocks Logic — That's the Point

Scammers create panic to stop you from thinking clearly. If you're feeling scared or confused, pause and ask someone you trust.

4. You're Never Alone — Always Talk to Someone

Before you share anything, talk to a parent, sibling, or teacher. Fear grows in silence — but disappears with advice.

5. Check the Number, Search the Case

If someone says they're from a police department, don't believe them blindly. Hang up and Google the department or call the official helpline to confirm.

☑ Red Flags of a Fake Police/Legal Scam:

- They say you're "under investigation" but can't explain why
- They ask for money, even as "security" or "clearance"
- They tell you not to talk to anyone
- They pressure you to act *immediately*
- They use WhatsApp calls or unknown numbers

Remember:

Real law doesn't hide behind phone calls.
Scammers sound serious — because they want you scared, not smart.

Be calm. Be alert.
And never fear asking for help.

---

15. The Digital Arrest Scam

(And How Students Can Protect Their Families)

Characters:

- *Dev* – 15, curious, into tech and news
- *Dev's Mom* – thoughtful but not very tech-savvy
- *Scammer* – posing as a "CBI official"
- *Dev's Dad* – appears briefly

[Scene: Dev is sitting at the dining table doing homework. His mom is on a WhatsApp call in the other room. Her tone suddenly turns anxious.]

Mom (on phone):
 Yes, officer… what do you mean a parcel in my name? No, I didn't send anything to Mumbai!
 Okay… I'm listening.

[Dev looks up, curious. His mom walks into the room, pale-faced.]

Dev:
 Maa? What happened?

Mom:
 Some officer from the Mumbai Cyber Cell just called. He said my Aadhaar was linked to an international drug

shipment. He sounded so official, Dev! He said it was a "digital arrest" and that I need to stay on the call.

Dev (suddenly alert):
 Wait—*digital arrest*? Did he say something about a parcel, or foreign currency?

Mom:
 Yes! And he's saying I'll be jailed if I don't cooperate. He wants me to verify my bank account now.

Dev (firmly):
 Maa, hang up. That's a scam. I've read about this — they target people using fear. They pretend to be police or CBI and call on WhatsApp to scare you.

Mom (confused):
 But Dev, he knew my name. He sent documents. It looked real...

Dev:
 They use fake ID cards, fake notices, even make video calls with people in uniform. But real police never call people like that — and never ask for account details over the phone.

[Dev takes her phone, hangs up, and blocks the number. He then shows her a news article on his tablet titled "Digital Arrest Scam: How WhatsApp Callers Are Tricking Indians."]

Dev:

 See? This is a common scam now. They keep people on video calls for hours, make them feel like criminals, and then ask for money to "verify accounts" or avoid arrest.

Mom:

 I was so scared... I almost sent them the bank details.

Dev:

 And that's exactly why they target people like you — calm, kind, but not very familiar with cybercrime. But that's why I'm here. We'll report it, and next time, you'll know.

[Later that night, Dev shares the same story with his dad at dinner. His parents agree to tell their friends and relatives too.]

❓ What Just Happened?

Dev's mom was nearly scammed by a "digital arrest" fraud — where criminals pretend to be police or government officers and use fear to manipulate victims.

They often say:

- "A parcel in your name was seized."
- "You're linked to criminal activity."
- "You're under digital surveillance."

- "Stay on the call or face legal action."

They dress like officials, use video calls, and send fake documents — all to make you panic.

 Real Incident:

In early 2024, an 86-year-old woman from South Mumbai became the victim of a horrifying cybercrime.
 She received a WhatsApp call from someone posing as a police officer, claiming her bank accounts were linked to an international drug cartel. They used phrases like:

- "This call is being recorded by Mumbai Police and RBI."
- "You're under digital surveillance."
- "You cannot disconnect the call, or a warrant will be issued."

Over two months, they convinced her that she needed to "cooperate" by transferring her money for investigation purposes.
 By the end, she had lost more than ₹20 crore — her entire life savings.

The fraud was so complex and psychologically controlling that she didn't speak to her family or friends during the entire period.

📚 Lesson: How to Spot a Digital Arrest Scam — And Teach Your Family

1. Real Police Don't Call on WhatsApp

Law enforcement follows official procedures — notices, court orders, police visits.
  They do not use WhatsApp, Telegram, or video calls to demand money or account info.

2. Fake Documents Look Real — But Aren't

Scammers use:

- Fake FIRs with your name
- Fake customs notices
- Photoshopped IDs with real logos

Always ask: Is this from a real source? Can I verify it independently?

3. Common Phrases Scammers Use: Real police will never say this.

- "This call is monitored by CBI and RBI."
- "You're under digital arrest."
- "This is a confidential investigation. Don't talk to anyone else."
- "Send ₹45,000 to verify your account or avoid jail."

4. If a Parent Gets Scared — You Can Step In

Teach your parents to:

- Hang up immediately.
- Never share OTPs, Aadhaar, or bank details.
- Call you or someone they trust before doing anything.

5. Report the Scam.

If your family receives such a call:

- Block the number
- Report it. (Check chapter 19).

☑ Quick Family Safety Tips:

- Help your parents turn on two-factor authentication.
- Add your number as an emergency contact for any digital issue.
- Explain that fear is a red flag — scammers want them scared.
- Practice what to do: hang up, screenshot, report.

Remember:

Scammers don't just target students — they target your parents, grandparents, and relatives.

Sometimes, the smartest thing a student can do is become the teacher.

You can protect your home by staying informed.
 You don't need a badge to fight crime — just the truth and a little confidence.

🧠 Final Thought

Scammers don't need to break into your house.
 They break into your mind — through fear, urgency, and fake authority.

But now you know:

- If it's urgent, scary, and makes you panic — pause.
- If it sounds official but comes through WhatsApp — hang up.
- If someone tells you not to speak to anyone — speak louder.

*Because no one has the right to arrest you digitally —
 and no lie is stronger than your ability to stop it.*

16. Group Pressure, Group Scam

Characters:

- *Aanya* – 16, sincere student, worried about upcoming boards
- *Rishi* – friend, confident, always has "inside info"
- *"EduX Cracker" Group* – a private WhatsApp group that promises exclusive study notes and test papers
- *Aanya's Mom* – appears later

[Scene: School break time. Aanya is sitting with Rishi, going through her physics notes with visible stress.]

Aanya:
  I swear, I'm not ready for this physics paper. These derivations are eating me alive.

Rishi (grinning):
  Relax. I've got a shortcut. I just joined this group called EduX Cracker — they're sharing paid test papers and topper notes. Direct PDFs. Board-focused.

Aanya (curious):
  Wait, what? How do you get in?

Rishi:
  You have to DM the admin and pay ₹299 — lifetime access. Everyone in tuition is in already.

Aanya:
 Is it safe? Like, who runs it?

Rishi:
 Some ex-IIT guy, apparently. Doesn't matter. The notes are ☑. People are scoring 90+ using these.

[Later that evening, Aanya scrolls through her DMs and finds the group invite link. The profile picture looks neat, the messages sound professional.]

Group Admin (message):
 📣 *Welcome to EduX Cracker. To activate access to the premium content, please UPI ₹299 to this number: 983xxx673. Screenshot required.*

[Aanya hesitates... but feels behind in studies. She pays. Sends screenshot. Gets "Access will be granted shortly."]

[Two hours later — nothing. Group deleted. Admin gone. Number blocked.]

Aanya (panicking):
 Wait... what? Where did the group go!?

[Next day, she finds Rishi.]

Aanya:
 Rishi, that EduX Cracker group vanished. They scammed me!

Rishi (awkward):
 What?! No way! But I saw messages yesterday...

Aanya:
 Did *you* even pay?

Rishi (quietly):
 No... I got the invite, but never sent money. Just thought it looked cool.

[Aanya tells her mom later that day, embarrassed.]

Aanya:
 I didn't want to worry you... but I paid for notes and it turned out to be fake.

Mom (gently):
 Beta, I know you're stressed. But these shortcuts? They're dangerous. Anyone can set up a group and pretend to be a genius tutor. You don't need to pay strangers to succeed.

❓ What Just Happened?

Aanya fell for a group scam disguised as academic help. These scams prey on exam pressure and FOMO (Fear of Missing Out). They create private groups that look exclusive, share sample content, and then lock access behind a "small fee."

Once enough students pay, they delete everything — and disappear.

 # Lesson: Don't Let Stress Lead to Scams

1. Just Because It's in a Group Doesn't Mean It's Legit

Scammers create Telegram/WhatsApp groups with fake names like:

- "Topper's Club"
- "Board Notes Hub"
- "EduCrack 2024"

They post some real-looking PDFs, fake reviews, and rush you to pay — then disappear.

2. Small Payments, Big Scams

Scammers target ₹99 to ₹499 amounts — small enough that students won't report, but large enough to steal from hundreds of people.

3. Who's Behind It? Ask Yourself:

- Is the admin verified?
- Can you find their name or credentials anywhere outside the group?
- Is there a real website, or just UPI numbers and vague promises?

4. Peer Pressure Makes Scams Seem Safer

When your classmates are doing it, it feels normal. But ask before you pay. Peer excitement is not proof.

5. Free Resources Already Exist

NCERT, CBSE official websites, YouTube educators, school teachers — you can find quality notes from verified sources. No need to pay unknown groups.

☑ Signs of a Group Scam:

- Payment through UPI only — no receipt, no legal proof
- No official teacher/admin identity
- Urgent messages like "Last chance to join!" or "Seats closing!"
- Group vanishes after payment
- You feel scared to ask questions

🧠 Remember:

Board pressure is real. But shortcuts from strangers can cost you more than marks.

Stay smart. Stick to sources you can trust.

---

17. Online Blackmail - "I Have Your Photo"

(You're Not Alone — And You're Not to Blame)

Characters:

- *Reeva* – 14, friendly, new to online chats and Instagram
- *"Dev"* – an anonymous user who seemed trustworthy
- *Aanya* – Reeva's cousin, older and emotionally strong
- *Reeva's School Counselor* – supportive adult who helps

[Scene: Reeva is sitting alone in her room, staring at her phone, hands trembling slightly. A message glows on the screen.]

Dev (DM):
 "I have your photo. If you don't send me more, I'll leak this one to your school friends. Don't test me."

Reeva (murmuring):
 I shouldn't have sent anything... I thought he liked me...

[Flashback: Two weeks earlier. Reeva started chatting with "Dev," a boy who followed her poetry account. He was kind, sweet, said she was beautiful. After many chats, he asked for a private selfie — just "for him." She sent a slightly edited, not-inappropriate photo — but still personal.]

[Present moment: Reeva doesn't reply. Her chest tightens. But instead of panicking, she walks to the living room, finds her cousin Aanya.]

Reeva (voice shaking):
  Di... I think I messed up. Someone I trusted is now threatening me. I sent a photo. Nothing bad. But still... I'm scared.

Aanya (calmly):
  Reeva. First — breathe. You didn't mess up. He did. You trusted someone. He broke it. That's not your shame — it's his crime.

Reeva:
  What if he sends it? I don't want people judging me...

Aanya:
  That's why we're not staying silent. We're reporting him. And I'm going to be right there with you.

[They go together to the school counselor. Reeva shares everything. The counselor reassures her, reports the account, and connects them to cyber support. No further messages come. Reeva never hears from "Dev" again.]

❓ What Just Happened?

Reeva faced a sextortion attempt — where someone emotionally manipulates you into sending a personal or private photo, then threatens to leak it unless you send more or do what they say.

It's one of the most dangerous and emotionally damaging scams — but also one of the most common.

Victims often:

- Feel ashamed
- Blame themselves
- Stay silent due to fear

Scammers use that silence as their weapon. But once the victim speaks up, the power shifts.

Lesson: What to Do If Someone Is Blackmailing You Online

1. Don't Respond. Don't Negotiate. Don't Apologize.

- You don't owe the scammer anything.

- Don't plead or panic — it shows fear, and they use that.
- Block them immediately. Take screenshots first.

2. You Did Not "Ask For It"

Whether you sent a personal photo or not — it's never your fault if someone misuses it.

Shame is how they control you. Awareness is how you stop them.

3. Never Pay or Send More to Make It Stop

- They'll only come back asking for more
- Even if they promise to "delete everything" — they won't

4. Report the Account Immediately

On Instagram, WhatsApp, Snapchat, Telegram — every platform has a report button. Check chapter 19 for other reporting mechanism.

5. Talk to a Trusted Adult — Even If You're Scared

It could be:

- Your older sibling
- Parent
- School counselor
- Teacher

You may feel nervous at first, but adults won't judge you — they'll protect you.

☑ Signs of a Sextortion Scam:

- Stranger builds trust quickly ("You're special", "You're different")
- Asks for personal photos "just for me"
- Suddenly becomes threatening or angry
- Uses fear of "leaking" as blackmail
- Refuses video calls or reveals little about themselves

Remember:

If someone says "I have your photo" — don't freeze.
Don't hide.
Act. Speak. Report.

Because no image, no message, no mistake...
should ever make you feel less than brave.

You're not the one in trouble.
You're the one taking your power back.

18: The eSIM Scam

(When Your Number Is Stolen Without Touching Your Phone)

Characters:

- *Ayaan* – 16, tech-enthusiast, uses an eSIM on his new smartphone
- *Zoya* – his friend, cautious and curious about digital security
- *Scammer (remote attacker)* – exploits leaked info to hijack eSIM
- *Ayaan's Mom* – affected when her eSIM was compromised

[Scene: Ayaan is explaining eSIM to Zoya after school.]

Zoya:
 Wait, what's an eSIM? Isn't that just a regular SIM?

Ayaan:
 Kind of. But no physical chip. It's built into the phone. You just scan a QR code from your telecom provider, and boom — number activated.

Zoya:
 So you can't lose it?

Ayaan:
 True. But it can be stolen digitally — that's the scary part.

[Flashback: A week earlier. Ayaan's mom got a message from her telecom company.]

"Your eSIM has been activated on a new device."

Mom (confused):
 But... I didn't activate anything.

Minutes later, her phone lost all network. WhatsApp logged out. UPI stopped working. Her Gmail password was reset.

[Ayaan helps her reach customer care. Turns out, someone had requested an eSIM transfer using her personal details — through email. No OTP, just basic info. They got the QR code and activated her number on a new phone.]

Ayaan:
 Someone literally *downloaded* your number onto their phone. Without ever touching your SIM.

❓ What Just Happened?

Ayaan's mom was a victim of an eSIM hijack — a newer version of SIM swap fraud.
 Instead of walking into a store and asking for a physical SIM, scammers request a digital eSIM transfer using leaked or stolen personal info.

They:

- Call/email the telecom company pretending to be you
- Say you've lost your phone
- Request a new eSIM QR code
- Receive it via email/SMS
- Activate your number on *their* phone

You lose network. They gain everything tied to your number.

Lesson: How eSIM Hijacking Works — And How to Stay Safe

1. What's an eSIM, Exactly?

An eSIM is a digital version of a SIM card, built into modern smartphones.
 Instead of inserting a physical chip, you activate your number using a QR code or digital profile.

Pros:

- Can't be physically stolen and useful while travelling
- Multiple profiles on one device

Cons:

- Can be hijacked remotely if someone impersonates you

- Often has fewer OTP protections if telecom companies are careless

2. Signs of eSIM Hijack

- Sudden loss of signal/network
- You stop receiving calls/SMS/OTPs
- You're logged out of WhatsApp, Gmail, or banking apps
- You receive a message like "Your eSIM has been activated" — and you didn't do it

3. How to Protect Yourself & Your Family

☑ Lock your telecom account
Ask your mobile provider to set a PIN or secondary password for any SIM or eSIM transfer

☑ Don't share personal info publicly
Scammers use DOB, email, and ID numbers to fake your identity

☑ Don't post your phone number online

☑ Especially on public forums, bios, or contest entries

☑ Use authenticator apps instead of SMS OTPs
This way, even if your number is hijacked, your 2FA codes stay safe

☑ Set up account recovery using email, not just mobile number

☑ Contact customer care immediately if you receive an eSIM activation message

4. What to Do if You're Hijacked

1. Call your mobile provider immediately from another phone
2. Ask them to block the eSIM profile and reissue your number
3. Change all passwords to email, banking, and social media accounts
4. Remove phone number as recovery on sensitive accounts
5. Enable 2FA using apps, not SMS
6. Report it. (Check chapter 19)

Remember:

With eSIM, the fraudster doesn't need to steal your phone. They just need to pretend to be you.

But if you stay alert, set proper security layers, and educate your family...
Your number — and your life — stays yours.

---

19. Cyber SOS: Know the Law, Save Yourself

Understanding Cyber Laws and Reporting Tools for Students

Characters:

- Ayaan – 16, tech-savvy, gamer, funny
- Tanya – 15, socially active, bold, has a large Instagram following
- Teacher (Ms. Sen) – digital literacy enthusiast

[Scene: After school, in the library. Tanya is looking worried, Ayaan walks in.]

Ayaan:
 Yo, Tanya. You okay? You've been off Insta all day — that's not like you.

Tanya (hesitant):
 Someone's been messaging me from fake accounts. First it was just comments… now they've DMed me threats. I blocked them, but they keep making new ones.

Ayaan:
 Whoa. That's serious. Did you report it?

Tanya:
 I didn't know what to do. Will the police even care?

[Ms. Sen walks by, overhearing them.]

Ms. Sen:
  They will care — and they *have to.* This is cyber harassment, and under Indian law, it's punishable.

 What's Happening to Tanya?

Tanya is being cyberstalked and harassed online — both are criminal offences under Indian cyber laws.

 Ms. Sen explains:

Ms. Sen:
We now have new criminal laws in India. The old IPC is being replaced by the Bharatiya Nyaya Sanhita (BNS), 2023 — but the protections remain. You are still fully protected from online abuse.

☑ Key Cyber Laws You Should Know (in simple words):

1. Section 66C & 66D (IT Act):
    Stealing your personal data, pretending to be you = punishable

2. Section 67 & 67A (IT Act):
   Sharing obscene images/content online = jail time and fine
3. Clause 73 (BNS):
   Cyberstalking — repeatedly contacting or tracking someone online = offence
4. Clause 131 (BNS):
   Sending threats anonymously or with intent to cause fear = crime
5. Clause 354 (BNS):
   Defamation — spreading false info to harm someone's image = punishable

---

☑ What Should You Do if You're Attacked Online?

Ms. Sen:
Remember this 5-step formula: SAVE.

S – Screenshot everything
Save proof before blocking. You'll need it to report.

A – Avoid responding
Don't reply to trolls or threats — it fuels them.

V – Verify privacy settings
Make your account private, remove unknown followers.

E – Escalate the issue
Block → Report to platform → Report to Cyber Crime → Inform someone you trust

---

⚖️ Where to Report in India?

1. Cyber Crime Portal: <u>www.cybercrime.gov.in</u>
   (24x7 national platform to file complaints — including anonymously)
2. Call 1930 (for financial frauds)
3. Local Police/Cyber Cell:
   File an FIR if it's serious — under BNS or IT Act
4. Child Helpline:
   📞 1098 (If you're under 18)

Tanya (relieved):
 I thought no one would take me seriously. But now I know what to do.

Ayaan:
 You're not alone. Next time someone hides behind a screen to scare you — show them you know your rights.

Ms. Sen (smiling):
 That's the spirit. The internet should feel safe. And if it doesn't — *you* have the power to change that.

Key Takeaways for Students

- Being harassed online is never "just a joke."
- Don't delete the proof. Save it. Screenshot everything.
- You have every right to report. No one is "too young" to be protected.
- Cyber safety is not optional — it's your right.
- New laws (BNS) + old laws (IT Act) = Full digital protection.

20. Final Chapter - Digital Defence

Your Story Starts With You

You've now seen the traps.

The fake jobs.
The flirty strangers.
The glowing giveaways.
The "police" who aren't really police.
The love that lies.
And the links that look real, but steal.

But you've also seen the power of one thing:

Awareness.

Not the kind in textbooks.
The kind that saves money.
That protects photos.
That guards your reputation, your family, your peace.

 So let's be honest:

Online scams aren't just "adult problems" anymore.
They're waiting in DMs.
They're pretending to be your friend.
They speak in emojis.
They promise easy marks, free phones, and quick love.

And they hope you won't notice — or worse, won't ask for help.

☑ But you're not helpless.

In fact, you're one of the strongest digital defenders around.

You're not just protecting your phone.

You're protecting:

Your younger siblings

Your parents who forward everything

Your friends who trust too easily

Your teachers who may not even know the scam exists

🧠 Use Your Brain Like a Firewall:

Pause before you click

Ask before you pay

Think before you trust

Tell someone before you feel trapped

Because the strongest tool you have... is you.

Your Role Now

You're not just a reader.

You're a digital first responder in your family.

You're someone others will come to — when their screen

shows something scary, shady, or strange.

Teach them what you've learned:

That fear is the scammer's favorite tool

That questions are powerful

That silence is where scammers grow

And that speaking up?

That's where it ends.

The End Is Just the Beginning

We're Just Getting Started...

You've reached the end of *Digital Defence - 1*, but in the ever-evolving world of the internet, learning to stay safe is a journey—not a one-time read.

If this book helped you think differently, stay alert, or share a tip with someone else, we'd love to know. Your thoughts matter. Your feedback will shape how we continue this mission—what worked, what didn't, and what *you* want to learn more about.

Got a story, question, or idea?
 Tell us! Your voice could inspire a future chapter.

Whether it's a scam you heard of, a strange message you got, or a doubt about something digital—don't keep it to yourself. Chances are, someone else is facing the same thing.

 Write to us at: feedbackcodes@gmail.com

 Be part of Digital Defence - 2. Let's build it together.

Stay sharp. Stay safe.
 — The Digital Defence Team